To:

From:

the I Love my life challenge

The Art and Science of Reconnecting
with Your Life: A Breakthrough Guide to
Spark Joy, Innovation, and Growth

ADAM MARKEL

IGNITE READS
spark impact in just one hour

simple truths
▶ Small books. BIG IMPACT.

Copyright © 2022 Adam Markel
Cover and internal design © 2022 by Sourcebooks
Cover design by Jackie Cummings
Internal images © endsheets, Esra Sen Kula/Getty Images; page vi, Henrik Sorensen/
Getty Images; page 24, Lynda Hinton/Unsplash; page 33, Magnus Olsson/Unsplash;
page 42, Westend61/Getty Images; page 47, Good Faces/Unsplash; page 50, Maskot/
Getty Images; page 58, LinkedIn Sales Solutions/Unsplash; page 63, Rawpixel/
Getty Images; page 66, LeoPatrizi/Getty Images; page 74, ThisisEngineering RAEng/
Unsplash; page 77, Joseph Gonzalez/Unsplash; page 80, Westend61/Getty Images;
page 83, nortonrsx/Getty Images; page 86, SDI Productions/Getty Images; page 89,
Randy Faris/Getty Images; page 92, urbazon/Getty Images; page 96, katleho Seisa/
Getty Images

Published by Simple Truths, an imprint of Sourcebooks
P.O. Box 4410, Naperville, Illinois 60567-4410
(630) 961-3900
sourcebooks.com

Printed and bound in the United States of America.
JOS 10 9 8 7 6 5 4 3 2 1

My wife, Randi, has been my rock.

My heart is filled with appreciation for my
partners, Randi, Deanna, and Chelsea;

and to Sourcebooks, and to my editor,
Meg Gibbons, for their great efforts
in bringing this vision to fruition.

Contents

The Power of Resilience

For many leaders, professionals, and individuals, the inability to respond to unexpected change can have dire consequences, ranging from despair to even suicide. Resilience provides an anchor through the storms of rapid change. It gives us the resolve to not just survive but thrive in challenging circumstances.

As a resilience expert, speaker, and author, I discovered a set of simple yet powerful questions that transformed my life and my clients' lives. The first of which is simply:

What if you decided to love your life no matter what?

This is why I created the I Love My Life Challenge: To live a fulfilled life no matter what. To lead your business and life with love no matter what. You meet this challenge by making mental shifts in a matter of seconds.

I know firsthand the devastation of burnout and the consequences of ignoring the shifting sands of the workplace. Twice I have found myself at a dead end in my career that I hadn't seen coming despite the warning signs. Each time, I brought myself back to life using the tools I share within this challenge.

If you can apply these small but powerful practices in the midst of the storm, you become the eye of that storm, and your calm becomes your greatest asset and ally. By unapologetically loving my life, no matter what, I raised myself to a new level of awareness, personal fulfillment, and success.

To be honest, you have to experience challenges in your life before you can love life.

One morning in 2017, I stood on a stage before a lively audience at a motivational training. The crowd included employees, managers, and CEOs. As with the hundreds of trainings I had led before, in just a few short hours, attendees moved from skepticism and impatience to excitement and joy.

But all morning, one man in the audience kept rolling his eyes and pursing his lips. He sat with crossed arms, and his legs fidgeted, as if he couldn't wait to leave the room. He never cracked a smile.

During the lunch break, I approached him and asked how he was doing.

He responded in a dismissive voice.

"I've been to these touchy-feely events," he said. "It may work for some people, but with all due respect, it's not my thing."

The "with all due respect" part threw me for a second, because I knew from my days as a litigator that respect was not really the intention.

To protect his privacy, let's just call this man

George. After a little probing, George let me know that he'd recently been through a divorce, health challenges, and a company downsizing. Now, at a new company, he wasn't sure he wanted to stay, because his job didn't give him the recognition or pay he felt he deserved.

Motivational events like this only made him *more* frustrated. "I won't drink the Kool-Aid," he said.

I knew I couldn't turn George around in the few minutes I had. I could only nod in agreement. Then I looked him in the eyes and threw out a buoy.

"George, here's a challenge for you," I said. "What if you decided to love your life, no matter what?"

He shifted uncomfortably in his seat. After lunch, I didn't see him again.

Six months later, I got an email from George. Since we met, his life had gone downhill. He went through a series of bad relationships. His job got worse. He slipped into depression.

"I just didn't know what else to do," he said. "Then

I remembered the question you asked me. What if I decided to love my life, no matter what? I decided right then and there I had nothing to lose. I'd take the challenge. I felt something change. Things started to get better. Your words changed my life. I haven't felt this good since as long as I can remember. *I really do love my life.*"

George's willingness to take on my challenge surprised me. What's more, the extent of the transformation he made astonished me. Once George made that mental shift—even after all his hardships—the universe responded to his belief.

I wanted to challenge others. When I spoke to leaders at business, industry, and personal-growth events, I started asking the same question: "What if you loved your life, no matter what?"

A few months after attending my events, people would reach out to me and share they were turning their businesses around, creating vibrant company cultures, enriching their relationships, improving their emotional well-being, and feeling more engaged and joyful in their lives.

I was humbled. Have you been hit by unexpected change? Has the change made it hard for you to fully love your life right now? You may have experienced massive upheaval—market disruption, business failure, job loss, divorce, or death of a loved one. Or maybe you're dealing with small, sometimes unavoidable, changes—technology, rules, expectations, to name a few. The relentless pace of change can be overwhelming. How can you be happy in the face of...uhhh, everything?

MAYBE YOU ARE

- ► *an overwhelmed professional or manager who must reinvent to stay relevant;*
- ► *a burned-out CEO or leader who has lost vision and direction; or*
- ► *an individual who just feels irrelevant and alone. You feel like you don't belong.*

MAYBE YOU ARE

▶ *working for someone you don't like, in a place you don't like; or*

▶ *caught up in achieving and striving, but you have no joy.*

AND MAYBE YOU FEEL

▶ *exhausted, burned out, depleted;*

▶ *fearful, doubtful, or worried;*

▶ *overwhelmed by the pace of change;*

▶ *disappointed, depressed, or even suicidal; and/or*

▶ *resigned and cynical.*

This sense of failure and lack of connection can erode your performance, exuberance, and love for life. With all the societal shifts going on, life seems to be changing faster than ever. Maybe you have a feeling that you too should change direction, but you don't know how. And you can't trust yourself to do it.

Or maybe something bad hasn't happened yet, but you know that if you don't act soon, your worst fears could be realized.

Looking at yourself as an individual and as a leader—of a business, profession, or your life—it is clear that your biggest risk is unexpected change. And the biggest challenge is whether you will face it by choice or default.

Living by choice keeps you agile, relevant, and feeling alive. It makes you resilient.

Living by default can lead to dissatisfaction and doubt.

With all the changes going on around us, sometimes the hardest thing to change is our own minds. But beliefs can be changed in a matter of seconds, and a life can be restored in a matter of hours and days.

This is your guide.

It's a way to quickly change your beliefs to become

a resilient leader. The key is learning to love your life, and in this book, I show you how.

After decades of incredible highs and devastating lows in my business, career, and personal life, I can say that I make this daily choice: I love my life, no matter what.

No matter what.

Since I made this shift, the blessings have flowed.

As a speaker and business strategist on the topic of resilience and reinvention, I have had the privilege of impacting the lives of millions of people. I've shared my message on stages of Fortune 500 and global corporations, including Oracle, Jack in the Box, JD Edwards, Henkel, and Herbalife. I've headlined with thought leaders like Michael J. Fox, Jack Canfield, and Sir Richard Branson.

I've also authored a bestselling book, *Pivot: The Art and Science of Reinventing Your Career and Life*, which took me to book signings and sold-out keynote speeches. As a resilience expert, I've been featured in *Forbes*, the *Wall Street Journal*, *USA Today*, and *Harvard Business Review*.

My TEDx talk, "Doing This for 10 Seconds Can Change Your Life," has been viewed more than two hundred thousand times. My podcast, *The Conscious Pivot*, and others I have spoken on have been downloaded more than one million times.

Since then, the legions of people who have taken on this challenge have reported astonishing, even miraculous results. As I said, the blessings have *flowed*. All these incredible moments and opportunities— these projects I have been able to be involved in and create—stem from my simple decision to love my life every day and learn and grow from that foundation.

This question serves as the anchor for myself in all I do: What if you loved your life, no matter what?

I never had a childhood dream of becoming the "I love my life" guy. In fact, I wanted to be a lawyer. Eventually, I did become a litigation attorney. Which is to say I challenged people in court for a living.

At the peak of my litigation career, I worked over seventy-hour weeks—for more than fifteen years. Then, I ended up in a hospital having what the doctor called an anxiety attack. At the time, it felt like I was having a heart attack. It was a huge wake-up call that resulted in a major pivot of my life. We uprooted our kids and left our home in New Jersey. We left our friends and family to move to California to run a new company. There was a lot of risk, but I ignored that and followed my heart into this new opportunity. My family supported that decision 100 percent, and off we went (more than somewhat blindly, I can say in hindsight).

My new position was CEO of a motivational training company, the largest in the world at the time. After working there for nearly two years, we expanded the business in more cities than before. I had also led dozens of weeklong trainings, resulting in thousands of people opening their minds and hearts for better businesses, careers, and lives.

By the summer of 2016, I had much to be grateful

for. The book *Pivot* was on the retail shelves and becoming a bestseller. My loving wife, Randi, was celebrating her fiftieth birthday. We had been married for twenty-seven years by then. And our second daughter, Lindsay, had just graduated college.

To celebrate, Randi and I, along with our four kids, enjoyed family time in Italy, then we flew to our favorite city—Paris. It should have been a fun, carefree time... but inside, I was a mess.

Over the last several months, the demands of promoting the book on national tours and giving extensive trainings—as well as leading a company as its CEO—had left me deeply depleted. In my heart, I knew I was on the verge of burning out. But I didn't want to admit it.

While in Paris, Lindsay asked me out to coffee for some father-daughter time. I sat with her in a small café on a narrow street off the Avenue des Champs-Élysées. I hoped that the strong French coffee would mask my exhaustion, but as we talked, Lindsay picked up on it right away.

"Dad," she said, "I'm really worried about you. You're doing it again."

"Doing what?" I asked.

"You're working too hard again. You're totally stressed out," she said. "I know you," Lindsay continued. "Here we are in Paris, and your mind is still on that job. We can still feel that you're stressed out even when we're on a family vacation."

She was calling me out and articulating my feelings that I hadn't had the courage to admit.

"Thank you for saying that," I said, and I took another sip of coffee. "It's funny how the universe works: when you write a book about pivoting, the universe sends you plenty of opportunities to become a master on that subject. It may be pivot time again."

But when I returned from Paris, I did what I had done before as a stressed-out lawyer. I ignored the warning signs. I put my head down and went back to working harder. Again.

In the following weeks, the warning bells sounded

even louder. Things weren't working with my business partners, who didn't see eye to eye with me on the direction of the company.

Still, I thought I could make it work. I thought I needed to make it work. What else would I do? Move back to New Jersey? Begin practicing law again?

A few months later, I traveled to Los Angeles for a six-day business training event. These programs were a roller-coaster mix of both the exhausting and the adrenaline-inducing. The sheer power of people transforming right before my eyes kept me going. It was a blessing to be a part of.

Once the event was completed, my partners (who had flown in from Asia) met me for lunch and proceeded to share their plans to take over the company. My role as CEO was being changed, and they said we'd discuss it at a later date.

As I absorbed what they said, I closed my eyes for a moment, and a calm voice inside me said, *Embrace the pivot.*

"Adam," said the director. "You're no longer the CEO. We'll find another role for you."

My body stiffened. I had been demoted.

I realized that my choice had been made by default. I had been forced into an outcome that my instincts had already known but I had not wanted to trust.

Within three months, I no longer had a job at the company.

After that meeting, I had a long and eerily quiet drive home. I walked into the house and sat alone in the dark. I thought, *I'm fifty-one years old. We have a mortgage. Bills. We still have kids to put through college. What the hell am I going to do?*

I felt that I had done everything I could. I had given my all. I had worked my butt off. My thoughts became a swarm of *would haves*, *should haves*, *could haves*, and *if onlys*.

In the months that followed, my emotions shifted. What gnawed at me now was a deeper anxiety that I couldn't put my finger on.

One morning, it hit me.

That sick feeling in my stomach wasn't really the worry about being able to provide for my family or being a victim of circumstance.

It was the fact that I was right back where I'd started.

The more I thought about it, the crazier it seemed. I'd been an angry, overworked, unhappy attorney. Then I'd left that to become—in the end—an angry, overworked, unhappy CEO.

It felt like I'd pivoted, reinvented myself, then somehow wound up right back where I started. I was living my own personal Groundhog Day.

Change. Stress. Change. Stress. Repeat.

A voice in my head whispered, *Why bother? You're just going to end up in the same place again.*

To make things worse, I was supposed to be the "pivot guy," the reinvention expert. I literally wrote the *book* on the subject. And yet here I was, a failed example of how to do just that. I felt like a hypocrite. I thought, *Was everything I stood for just a sham?*

At that moment, everything felt transitional, like ethereal dust. I was discouraged, overwhelmed, and losing hope every day.

I had every reason to hate life for being so cruel.

But I didn't.

Perhaps it was the work I had been doing for so many years pointing others in the direction of hope that buoyed me in that moment. But whatever it was, I knew the game wasn't even close to over. Dealing with myself honestly yet lovingly was what I needed to move forward.

Over the years, I'd built a very consistent ritual into my mornings. The ritual is a simple series of practices that I do almost every day. They ground me and help me prepare—mentally, emotionally, and spiritually—for the day ahead.

This ritual always begins the same way: I sit up in bed each morning, I put my feet on the floor, and I say, "I love my life."

I've been doing it so long, the ritual transformed

into something automatic. It's a habit. So even as I was swirling down the vortex of despair, I would wake up in the morning, and almost without thinking, I'd say, "I love my life."

One morning, just after my feet landed on the floor, I wondered for the first time if it was actually still true. Was I just saying it, or did I truly love my life? Was I just trying to convince myself?

The answer came immediately. *Yes.* I knew I loved my life. At least some of it.

I imagined waking up in the morning and saying, "I love the good parts of my life, but everything else sucks."

I wanted no part of that.

I knew intuitively that I had to love all of my life. The ups and downs. The unexpected twists and turns and roadblocks. For better or worse—as I had vowed to my wife decades ago. Now, such a vow would need to be to myself.

It was a new perspective, which brought a new

sense of freedom, and it happened in a matter of seconds. No years of therapy or months of training. Like a drowning swimmer finally taking a breath of air, I could breathe again. I was alive.

When the morning grew brighter, I laced up my sneakers and put my earbuds in my ears. I walked out the front door of my house to figure out the future.

As I walked along the beach, I listened to an audiobook that had hit number one on bestsellers lists. Thousands of people had told me the book had completely transformed their lives. Now, it was my turn to listen.

I cringed as I heard my own voice announce the title: *Pivot: The Art and Science of Reinventing Your Career and Life*. Despite being the author, I had never listened to the book I had written and narrated. Talk about excruciating. Yet here I was, listening to myself give advice about reinventing my life.

But as I walked, I started to feel its truth.

I did a lot of walking that week. I walked by myself.

I walked with the dogs. I walked the beach, the trails, and the streets.

In my time alone, I started to look at myself with radical honesty and reframe my experiences. I gained insights and created a new vision of my life going forward. My spirit was recharged.

As I affirmed how much I loved my life—even through the failures—I felt an infusion of energy. A stronger sense of resilience.

By the end of listening to my own story, which included my own techniques for change, I knew two things for sure.

The first was that despite what my anxiety-fueled brain had been telling me, *Pivot* was something I was proud of. I believed in it, and it worked. And I knew it worked because by the end of the book, I had a plan in place.

The second thing I knew was that in my life, the big changes had derailed me because I hadn't paid enough attention to the small changes along the way. I was too exhausted to keep up with the pace of change. That's why I kept landing on repeat.

I was learning to love my life again. I was learning to restore myself and come into my own. I was gaining insight as a resilient leader of my life and business.

I knew I would build resilience in the face of persistent setbacks. I would explore how to remain relevant in the face of big changes as well as in the face of the small, persistent changes that show up each day.

In the months that followed, I started to make small changes that led to a miraculous new direction. One of those small changes was actually slowing down and not rushing to fill the space that was left when the business I had been nurturing was taken away. Slowing down became a buoy for me to hold on to when my instincts were to rush to fix what had broken.

By the end of that year, I no longer felt like a hypocrite. When I observed my morning rituals, I knew that my words and actions aligned with the deepest parts of my spirit.

In the mornings, when I woke up and touched my feet to the ground, I could say with complete authenticity: "I love my life, no matter what!"

What if you too could move beyond resilience to *thriving*? From simply getting by to *flourishing*? What if you were to take on the challenge of loving your life, *no matter what*?

When you lead with love—in any area of your life—you become a resilient leader. You are able to recharge, innovate, and anticipate change at faster rates than ever before. You stay on the growth edge, able to sail with the winds of change rather than against them.

Whether the changes are big or small and persistent, you're able to move seamlessly, using love as your calibrator.

Hundreds of thousands of people have accepted this challenge, and they've transformed their lives. In as little as ten seconds, they start their days with joy. They navigate obstacles and become resilient leaders in their lives. They love their lives. No matter what. No BS.

Now, it's your turn.

By taking on the I Love My Life Challenge, you have a greater sense of fulfilling your life mission. More than ever, you trust yourself, understand your journey, and appreciate your destiny. You regain your sense of mastery and awe. Even through the worst of times, you authentically embrace your life with love.

You wake up every morning, touch your feet on the ground, take a deep breath, and truthfully say, "I love my life!"

CHAPTER ONE

Not on My Watch

The summer I was nineteen years old, I worked as an ocean lifeguard at Jones Beach, on Long Island, New York. One day, I started my shift like all the others I had completed before. Perched on my lifeguard stand, I scanned the beach's historic tower; the crisp, blue ocean that went miles into the distance; and the hundreds of families in my beach area. Even as I heard the sound of people laughing and children squealing, I kept watch to make sure people stayed safe. As a first-time lifeguard, I was excited and proud to be there.

Later on in my shift, while I was scanning the area, I heard three short, sharp whistles pierce the air. *Missing swimmer.* I scrambled down the lifeguard stand and ran toward Captain Bob, who had sounded the rescue alarm.

"They lost someone at Field 3. It's a search and rescue," said Bob. "Go!"

Ten of us lifeguards ran down the beach to join the search team. A crowd had formed, and people were pointing to where they last saw the missing swimmer. We hurried into the ocean water; it was foaming like a washing machine. Our group of lifeguards formed a straight line perpendicular to the shore and started the search pattern. As a group, we dove down into the cold, dark water and swam into the current. This way, a drowning body would be moving toward us, not away.

When all the lifeguards' heads popped up out of

the water, we repeated the pattern again, and again, and again.

In the cold, dark water, I swam with my arms outstretched, hoping to touch a body, yet terrified at the same time that I might find them. We were exhausted and wracked from the cold, but we didn't come in.

After over an hour, we moved to another part of the beach, still searching for the body. Then Captain Bob's whistle blew again, calling us to shore. It was an awful, sinking feeling—*We weren't done yet; we hadn't found him!*

As we huddled around Captain Bob on the beach, my body shivered. My legs and arms were numb, and my fingers and toes were like prunes from being in the water so long.

"Let's bow our heads in a moment of silence," said Captain Bob, "for the missing man and his family."

When we opened our eyes again, Captain Bob said, "No one goes down in our water. At this beach, no one—not one more soul—goes down on our watch," he declared. Then he said something I will never forget: "You either make the save, or you die trying!"

Those words became my mantra as well as my protection, my guard, my shield. *No one goes down on my watch.*

In my next seven years as a lifeguard at that beach, no swimmer ever went missing again. For years, that mantra—that belief—gave me strength. It helped me protect my business, my clients, my employees, my family, and myself...*until it didn't.*

Eventually, I saw that my belief had become my prison.

If I never left my watch, no one would go down in my water. Time and again—one crisis after another—I never came in. Instead, I was the one left drowning. I had lived guarded and on guard. All that guarding did was leave me depleted and unfulfilled, just like that day at the beach when I was nineteen, when we couldn't save that missing swimmer.

I saw that every change I had made—job, company, industry, city—brought me back to the same state of deep exhaustion. I had been living by my belief: *You either make the save, or you die trying.*

I finally saw that this old mantra no longer served me. I understood that I could let it go. At the same time, I took on a new belief: *I love my life, no matter what.*

As I let go of my old belief and embraced this new one, my life shifted. My exhaustion turned into restoration. My fears turned into possibility. I found myself resilient to not just the big changes in my life but also the small, persistent changes that had taken me off course.

In the weeks and months that followed, I found that I was no longer feeling guarded. Now I was feeling guided instead—no longer living on guard but living in grace.

Have you ever had a belief that worked until it didn't? These kinds of beliefs seem to work perfectly in your life—taking you to great heights of success and accomplishment—until you realize they are costing too much.

It seems easy enough to change our beliefs. We change our *minds* all the time—about our shoes, our favorite coffee, and even our goals.

Yet changing *beliefs* can seem impossible. An entire continent of leaders tortured the first man to say that the earth revolves around the sun. The suffragettes went to jail for challenging existing voting laws.

In the I Love My Life Challenge—when you commit to loving your life no matter what—the real challenge is letting go of beliefs that no longer serve you.

I want you to let go of these old ideas and mantras before you become as miserable as I was. You shouldn't have to hit bottom to know that you're off course. Identifying and letting go of outdated beliefs gives you the space to embrace new ones. Your new beliefs allow you to live by choice instead of by default. They give you vision, resilience, and the opportunity to create a return on investment—what I like to call a harvest.

When you take on this challenge, you are committing to live in this new belief. With the steps I show you, you will be able to walk this path and strengthen your resilient leadership, and it will only take ten seconds at a time. In business and life, loving your life gives you the resilience to face any change—whether big or small—while anticipating the future.

When someone is missing at sea, ten seconds can make the difference between breathing and drowning, between life and death.

No matter your situation, a few moments can make the difference between life and death, because that's all it takes to grab a mental buoy and change your beliefs.

At their worst level, beliefs that don't serve us can lead to despair, isolation, and even suicide. Our despair is epidemic. The irony is no matter how isolated we feel, we are suffering as an entire society. From CEOs to teens, our levels of pain sound an urgent wake-up call. There's more than enough research to know people are anxious—and even anxious about their anxiousness. Sleep aids of all kinds are proliferating right alongside antidepressants, and at least one in four people surveyed between the ages of eighteen and twenty-four considered taking their own life in June 2020.

As it did with me, the symptoms can range from exhaustion to hopelessness and depression. For others, it can mean resignation and bitterness. In the United States, this has manifested in alarming rates of obesity, opioid addiction, and suicide.

American CEOs are suffering what BEST Life and Health Insurance Company calls "the financial post-traumatic stress syndrome," with outcomes ranging from depression to suicide. According to *Forbes*, the suicides of high-profile entrepreneurs such as Kate Spade, Anthony Bourdain, Jody Sherman, and Ilya Zhitomirskiy shed light on the underlying feelings that many entrepreneurs experience: "high-stress life, enormous uncertainty, exhaustion, and risk of

humiliation." This boils down to "the feeling of entrapment," from which suicide becomes a dangerous fantasy of freedom.

Suicide rates have also jumped for working adults. Since the late 1990s, the suicide rate has increased by one-third for career-prime adults ages forty-five to sixty-four, according to Pacific Standard. According to the National Institute of Mental Health, suicide is now the leading cause of death for those under age thirty-four. Due to how overwhelming this issue has become, we have included additional resources in the appendix to help you if you are experiencing suicidal thoughts. Please stop reading now and flip to page 101 if this even somewhat sparks true to your experience.

Even in high-tech industries, a quarter-life crisis can hit by age thirty. Because of rapidly changing technology, these workers feel obsolete at younger and younger ages, said an expert quoted in a *New York Times* article. Add to that student debt, job losses due to artificial intelligence, and a volatile environmental climate, and the sense of helplessness can become overwhelming.

In the new disruptive economy, corporations are also at risk. Of the Fortune 500 companies from the year 2000, more than half—exactly 52 percent—were out of business by 2018.

According to the 2019 World Happiness Report—coauthored by bestselling author and economist Jeffrey Sachs—Americans' overall happiness continues to decline. This is because Americans are experiencing less "social support," as the United States turns into a "mass-addiction society."

As a society, we're taught to "live to fight another day." However, if we want to live, it's time to change that. Instead, we need to "live to *love* another day."

When we lead with love, we serve as role models to others. We can reset our minds, emotions, bodies, and spirits to restore ourselves and become masters of our lives. We can lead our businesses and teams to create cultures of loving resilience.

When you have the tools and skills of a resilient leader, you can anticipate changes and craft better outcomes. By making easy, positive micro changes, you diffuse and prevent devastating, negative macro changes.

Change itself is not bad. In the history of life on earth, it's not the biggest or strongest who survive; it's the ones who can most quickly adapt, the ones who stay relevant over time. As a human species, we've always faced change. We've always found a way to overcome obstacles and emerge stronger. That's resilience.

Resilience draws on the inner strength we all have, and it provides an anchor through the storms of rapid change. It gives us the grit to not just survive but thrive in challenging circumstances.

As a former lifeguard, I know that best practice is to stock a boat with life jackets before setting sail. In the same way, resilience is something you create before you need it. It means planning for disruption before it happens, reinventing before you get the ax, and innovating before you become irrelevant. By culti-vating resilience, you make yourself immune to change.

I no longer believe my role is to save people, at least in the literal sense, but I can show you how to rescue yourself.

If you're ready to commit, you're holding the resources you need in your hands. This book is your guide. It's a personal journey, but you're not alone. You're part of our community of clients and individuals who have taken it on and achieved incredible results.

This challenge to love your life no matter what happens mostly in your mind and heart, but I give you practical and tangible tools you can use daily to help you along the way. Each concept and every tool is meant to strengthen you as a resilient leader. Your ultimate goal is to love your life, regardless of the challenges.

Before we begin, I invite you to test your resilience. The Resilience Assessment Tool allows you to measure your resilience and progress. This peer-reviewed assessment tool gives you a starting point. Go to resiliencerank.com to take your test, or scan the QR code on this page!

You can also use this assessment tool to strengthen your team and develop a culture of resilience. That way, self-care and resilience are not just a credo but a way of life. Culture is created through leadership, not the plaque in the break room. Be the model and cultivate resilience in your company.

Scan me with a camera phone for more content!

When you're done with your assessment, you will receive an email from our team with your assessment results and a resilience kit to begin making valuable changes.

Go ahead. Do it now.

Each person's journey is unique.

As you read, you may feel called to certain chapters. You may want to jump to sections that seem most relevant to your life now. Or you may want to return to some chapters you've already read to absorb ideas more deeply and make mental shifts, just ten seconds at a time.

Consider this your private cruise to self-improvement and resilience. You control the navigation.

PART ONE

Recover Yourself

Love yourself first and everything else falls into line. You really have to love yourself to get anything done in this world.

—LUCILLE BALL

CHAPTER TWO

Radical Honesty

Radical honesty is about facing the truth of what's not working. It's about moving from fear and denial to making more conscious choices and decisions. In business, it means telling the truth about your market, your industry, your company, and your job. It means clearly facing business challenges, anticipating future trends, and finding ways to innovate—before someone else forces you to change.

In life, it's about inviting feedback and then

consciously choosing to change. I've lied to myself many times—perhaps you can relate to that as well. I'm convinced we do it to feel safe. My self-deceit was on display, but of course I was unconscious of it, since life had been going pretty well. My chosen profession was paying handsome dividends in the form of power and prestige, not to mention more money than my family had ever seen before. Lawyering was something I seemed well-suited for—I was paid to argue and reconcile, to break down and build back up. It was a seemingly constant series of melodramas to participate in and profit from. Things were going my way, so at first it was hard to notice the signs that my soul was uneasy. The disturbances in the universe that was my life—as a husband, father, and business owner—were subtle yet seeable. I kept the signposts to myself.

Baseball was on my mind when I was driving to our son's Saturday morning game, but the signposts actually led me to the emergency room where nurses assisted me onto a gurney and stuck electrodes to my chest.

The heart is our home base, and mine was ticking so fast and hard that I could barely catch my breath. The signs were now obvious to others, and any attempt to hide them from myself or them was futile. Self-loathing was my bed companion in the moments waiting for the doctor. *How could I have ignored it for so long? I can't believe I won't see my kids again. How could I do this to my wife?*

Radical honesty ultimately frees you. The hardest place to start on the path to honesty is with ourselves. It's simply easier to tell ourselves what we want to hear or what we think will make us feel better than what is ultimately truthful about what's going on. The issue with this kind of benevolent mendacity is that it creates blind spots. These blind spots shield us from reality and keep us from fully utilizing our keen senses and loving awareness to collect the feedback that is all around us. Without that feedback, it is so much harder for us to learn and grow; therein lies our dilemma. *Without growth, we perish.*

Honesty that begins with ourselves embraces reality and all the opportunities for growth that it presents. Honesty isn't about telling the truth, it's about *living* the truth, embodying self-awareness that is loving and not judgmental. Honesty is not another tool to use to beat yourself or other people up. It's a resource to conquer fear and liberate the power of your being. In business and entrepreneurial pursuits, radical honesty is being someone who stands for things that matter without apologies or excuses. It is speaking your own truth with compassion and empathy instead of brutality. It is modeling leadership as you would want to be led yourself.

There's one central question that I ask my colleagues and clients in both business and personal contexts: "What's the most honest communication possible in this moment?"

When that question is asked and answered transparently, the result is powerful authenticity that draws people closer. What more can you ask of yourself as

a leader than to connect and create a union with others?

When the doctor finally slid the curtain back to see me in my state of distress, he (thankfully) told me that I wasn't having a heart attack. Instead, he said I was experiencing a panic or anxiety attack that felt as if it was a heart attack. He said my issue was likely stress and the lack of proper attention to myself. When I shared my recent history of sleep issues, work challenges, and the copious amount of coffee I was drinking to push through the day, he just nodded. Before he discharged me and told my wife that she could take me home, he looked my way and said, "You'll be okay, but you have to be more honest with yourself and consider making some changes." Those words were a reprieve and buoy for me to hold on to as I navigated the unknown depths of radical honesty.

In business and in life, we have to own what's ours. We have the opportunity each day to unflinchingly and courageously take more personal responsibility for what is ours to own. It helps to even ask that question aloud: "What's mine to own?" When we find that we've made mistakes, we can do something that can only raise the bar as a leader. We can embrace these six simple words: "I was wrong, and I'm sorry."

Here's what to do: Put a structure for change in place—before change is forced on you. Cultivate a leadership style that allows for bold self-reflection. Ask yourself, *What's the most honest communication possible in this moment?* Ask yourself, *What's mine to own?*

CHAPTER THREE

Reframe

We constantly face crises. On both professional and personal levels, we meet challenges and setbacks daily. You can shift a crisis to an opportunity by reframing the situation. This means seeing challenges differently. It means changing your perspective without having to change the circumstances. Reframing allows you to detach from a challenge so you can find the longer term opportunity for growth.

On April 19, 2018, two men were waiting to conduct a business meeting at a Starbucks in Philadelphia, Pennsylvania, when they were arrested. The details of the incident reported to police were almost unimaginable: two African American men were removed from the Starbucks in handcuffs after asking to use the restroom and waiting for a business associate to arrive for a meeting.

Imagine that you are the CEO of Starbucks receiving the call that a manager at one of your stores just violated the civil rights of two patrons. What do you do? Who do you call next? What advice do you ask for from legal counsel, your public relations folks, and the director of human resources? You can imagine the CEO would be advised to distance the company from the event and throw the "rogue" manager under the bus as quickly as possible. The legal ramifications could be massive, and the public stock price could take a substantial hit; it could even cost the shareholders millions of dollars.

So what did Kevin Johnson, CEO of Starbucks, say and do in response?

He stepped back and reframed the situation.

Reframing is the most important thing we can do to create a positive psychology for ourselves in times of radical change and disruption.

There are essentially three steps to reframing. When faced with an uncertain situation—especially one that threatens our well-being, safety, or security in some way—we must *pause*, *ask*, and *choose*.

Pausing is moving our thinking and emotional response to neutral. Just as we can shift our car's transmission into neutral, we must shift ourselves into a state that is not in gear. Essentially, that means being present in the situation without giving it meaning. This is hard to do since we are meaning-making machines. However, we must shift to look at things without adding our judgments of *right or wrong*, *good or bad*, and *fair or unfair* and simply see the event or circumstance as something neutral.

In that state of neutrality (the pause), you can ask questions and explore what there is to discern.

Asking questions to find answers may be thought of as having a cause-and-effect relationship. My own experience is that one always gets an answer to a question at some point. What defines the quality of the answer, however, is the quality of the question. In a neutral state that we create from pausing, we can ask better questions, questions that dive deeper to find meaning in the circumstances. This deeper meaning is something my grandmother Edith used to call "little gems."

One of the questions that can get you to little gems is to ask "What is the creative opportunity presented in this moment?" My wife, Randi, asks me this question all the time, but especially when things have gone differently than expected and when there's some disappointment. Once we have obtained those nuggets of wisdom, we can take the third step in any reframe, and that is to choose. *Choosing* becomes easier and more clear as a result of the questions and answers that precede any decision-making efforts.

Johnson was faced with a clear dilemma in responding to the calls of the press and markets. Was Starbucks a racist organization? Was he a racist himself for allowing the company to discriminate against black and brown customers? Enter the reframe.

Instead of seeing the threat as something inherently bad or wrong or unfair or requiring denial, deflection, and distancing, Johnson went on live television the morning after the event and answered questions from *Good Morning America* anchor Robin Roberts. He didn't deny the incident nor do anything to blame the manager or justify what occurred. He simply told the truth and owned the company's part in having an incident of bias and discrimination occur on their watch. He was succinct and open. He shared that he didn't know enough to explain how the event occurred, but he promised to get to the bottom of it and make whatever changes were needed to correct Starbucks' course.

Within a few months, Starbucks had resolved the dispute with the men who were wrongfully harassed and arrested. Johnson closed eight thousand stores nationwide for four hours of training on unconscious bias at a cost of approximately $11 million dollars. Johnson found the creative opportunity to stand for something in a vulnerable and transparent way, and stakeholders and the public responded favorably to that leadership. Since this event, other companies like Sephora have encountered unconscious bias in their workplaces, and they've drawn on the example and blueprint that Starbucks modeled as a way to find the little gems in those instances where communication and empathy had broken down. While there is still a lot of work to be done by all, cutting out the immediate defenses and taking proactive actions to be the change we are looking for are good first steps.

Instead of reacting to crisis, resilient leaders ask, "What's the creative opportunity here?" And then they take action. In your business and life, take an inventory of the obstacles, and reframe each one. In the coming pages, I'll show you how to turn them into creative opportunities.

CHAPTER FOUR

Re-vision

In business and life, we can become so overwhelmed in the experiences of living that we lose the lessons. To regain the meaning in our lives, we need to create a powerful new vision. This requires us to mine insights from our past to take us into the future.

My tailspin from my career in law left me a bit dizzy and certainly confused about my path forward. It didn't seem to make sense at the time. I had accomplished my goal of graduating law school and passing the bar exam, starting a private practice, and even making plenty of money for years.

Why was I feeling unhappy and unfulfilled? This question led me to the proverbial soul-searching that can be a harbinger of change. I didn't have much spare time back in those days, but I remember sinking into a few books that opened my mind, including the classic *The Road Less Traveled* by Dr. M. Scott Peck.

I realized as I was reading that there were signs in my life that I hadn't been paying attention to. There was writing on the wall that I was actually ignoring. One of those signposts was the feeling of shame that I had for being so money driven and cutthroat in my work. These feelings were tough for me to handle, and they filled me with even greater angst. I remember coming home late from work one evening—it was one of those cold, rainy East Coast nights—and I walked into our house dripping wet. I looked at my wife, who was heading upstairs, and her face said it all—I realized I had missed the kids for dinner again, and now I was missing the opportunity to read to them and kiss them good night as well. This was not the first miss on my part, and I felt instantly disgusted with myself. I don't even know what took over in that moment, but I looked into the eyes of my college sweetheart and said, "If I keep doing what I'm doing, you're going to be a widow."

Right now, people all over the world are facing both new and old challenges. In the wake of the COVID-19 pandemic, anxiety and depression have risen to levels not recorded since the Great Depression. Uncertainty is ever present, and many people are being fed a regular cocktail of extremely disheartening news about the environment, politics, business, and global health. It's time for a collective deep breath and some tangible strategies to move forward without exacerbating the drama that seems baked into the cake of everyday life for so many.

Pivoting has become a term of art during these times of radical change, so it makes sense to refer back to and supplement some of the lessons in my last book, *Pivot: The Art and Science of Reinventing Your Career and Life*. One of the most important insights I have gained as a husband, father, and business owner has been to develop resilience—for myself and for my family (my literal family and the team members of our companies). Resilience is its own deep-dive concept, which I speak about in my keynote speeches to organizations and during each episode of *The Conscious Pivot* podcast, but there's one aspect that cannot be ignored in the current world context: *vision*. More specifically, our ability to adapt and revise our vision to resemble the fast-growing and flexible willow tree.

Our ability to "re-vision" our course is the surest way I know to stay relevant and valuable to ourselves and others when the winds of change are blowing the fiercest. To re-vision, we must first revisit the experiences we have had and are having to find the common threads and breadcrumbs of wisdom and guidance for the future.

I could see that the comment I made to my wife

shook her. She took a deep breath, stared straight into my eyes, and said, "We'll figure it out." I knew in that moment, as I have always known, that she had my back and would not abandon me when I was at my most vulnerable.

Before I knew what to do, I knew what not to do. I didn't propose closing my business or moving to a beautiful island to escape the reality of the situation. Like a kid learning to bowl, I needed some guardrails to keep my thoughts from rolling into the gutter. Randi and I decided we would take some time to think about what might be possible. We went to one of our favorite places that we also call "our haven," and we walked and walked. We might have had a bottle of wine at one point as well. We also prayed together for guidance. It wasn't a thunderbolt of lightning, but I could feel a jolt of energy in me that hadn't been there in a while. I could see that there were options—a lot of them! When we got home, I decided to find an office in our town that was close to our home, and I would only commute to New York City three days a week at first. That would save me eight hours of travel time per week—and I could be home for dinner and bedtime at least two nights per week. Suddenly, there was a clearing in the sky of my clouded thoughts and a new vista in my view.

When we deliberately look for insights in our lives, consciously finding the wisdom in our experiences, we can let go of past challenges. We are no longer at the mercy of the winds, waters, and weather patterns of life. The new vision we create charts a new course for the future. We are tacking into the wind, creating intentional progress and direction.

CHAPTER FIVE

Recharge

Recharging is our default state of being—until we learn how not to take ourselves for granted. Recharging is a mandate to recover. It's a way to return to our natural rhythms, so we can refuel the tank and rehab the motor. Recharging happens at all levels: physical, mental, emotional, and even spiritual. The goal is to renew, refresh, and regenerate, spawning fresh ideas and capacity for more. Whether on a business, career, or personal level, recharging strengthens us as teams and individuals.

Have you ever seen *Rocky*—the first film in the Rocky franchise? It was released in 1976. There are only a few films from my childhood that I remember so well. When *Jaws* filled me with fear, *Rocky* filled me with courage. Sylvester Stallone plays a professional fighter who gets knocked down again and again—perhaps too many times to count—and in every single instance, he gets back up. The sheer will to stand tall in the face of adversity is enough to stand and cheer for, which is what we all did when the movie ended. It spilled out of the theater and into the street afterward. I was just a kid, but my dad could hardly contain me as I burst out of the theater, ran down the middle of the street, and hummed the theme song "Gonna Fly Now" as I punched my arms toward the sky!

From the time we're kids, we all want to be the superheroes of our own lives. We think we're invincible for a long time. We give it our all and put so much on the line, while we adopt the philosophy of a warrior on the field of play (and battle) in our daily lives. *Rocky* gave us a blueprint for the tenacity and grit required to not stay down, no matter how many times we suffer disappointment and loss. But if we never stay down, never recover, and just keep on fighting...what does it cost?

Harvard Business Review reported the findings of Jim Loehr and Tony Schwartz in "The Making of a Corporate Athlete." The research compared the performance of highly successful Olympic and professional athletes with highly successful corporate executives. Surprisingly, they found they had one thing in common—rituals around rest.

Yes, *rest.*

Across the board, the individuals shared rituals they created and maintained to recover and recharge mentally, emotionally, physically, and even spiritually (sometimes referred to as MEPS). Over time, what has been proven to me, while using factor analysis and our assessment of thousands of individuals, is that resilience is not about how you endure but how you *recover*.

Therefore, success is less about winning a night-owl award and more likely the result of solid habits and rituals that ensure that renewal practices are equal to or greater than the rate of exertion and exhaustion. Burnout, it has been found, is the result of ignoring recovery and *running on empty*. The opportunity to come back to ourselves more quickly leads to greater capacity across the MEPS spectrum. Learning to ritualize and habitualize our self-care becomes the basis of our own self-rescue.

Rocky is a wonderful story. We can't help but root for Sly Stallone to get up each time he's knocked to the canvas. He's the superhero we all think we have to be on some level. But even though he wins our hearts in the movie, he loses the fight. And he "don't look too good" in the end either.

Be it a morning meditation, an afternoon recap and to-do list drafting session, or whatever method of self-care and taking a beat you prefer, the best way to recharge your business and life on a daily basis is through rituals and rest.

PART TWO

Come into Your Own

Always remember,
your focus determines
your reality.

—GEORGE LUCAS

CHAPTER SIX

Agility

The rudders of a ship allow it to make small turns that can eventually change the entire direction of the vessel—but that's just the beginning of the story. When larger and larger ships were being constructed, there was an unanticipated issue: the ships couldn't turn quickly or easily, which made them both dangerous and impractical. The bigger the rudder that was developed, the more profound the issue became. It wasn't until a relatively tiny rudder, called a trim tab, was affixed to the large rudder to assist it in turning that these behemoth boats became agile. In our businesses and lives, when we make small turns or micro changes, we have the capacity to move larger objects and avoid dangers before it's too late to turn. *This is agility.*

We don't often understand that being agile doesn't require us to go all in or make huge commitments. All that is required is an openness to recalibrate when circumstances or opportunities invite change. Recalibration is something each of us can do from wherever we find ourselves and no matter the situation.

My wife and I hadn't been married long before the kids starting arriving. What a blessing it was to be a father. One Father's Day early in my dad tenure was memorialized by a photo album and a poem. My dearest Randi has always been somewhat crafty and creative. To this day, she astounds me when she puts her thoughts into verse, and on this occasion, she floored me yet again. She titled the poem "Divisionman." Stanza by stanza, she unpacked the tale of a person

capable of leaping tall buildings (like a kids' pillow fort) in one moment while negotiating a contract dispute in the next. Someone who was capable of making French toast for the family breakfast and drawing pictures of sailboats for a huddled mass of kindergartners before writing legal briefs and then creating elaborate bedtime stories later that night. Divisionman even sprinkled in the occasional round of golf or dash to see a beach sunset for good measure.

The poem was about the ability to utilize and even bend time to suit the requirements of a life that wanted to suck the marrow from each passing day. The through line was and still is agility. As I look back on those years of raising kids and raising a business at the same time, I realize how agile I was. I didn't get taken out by how much there was to do or the dreaded hows of getting it all done. I simply recalibrated during each day—I made micro pivots again and again—focusing intently on what was in front of me for short intervals before inviting a change to my attention.

In discovering my own optimal performance zone, one thing was clear: agility was my superpower. I truly was Divisionman, as Randi wrote so many years ago.

In the world we have before us, agility means planning for change in advance and having the flexibility to improvise and innovate before we are forced to.

Buckminster Fuller used to refer to trim tabs as a metaphor for living and leading. We are just like those little rudders that are able to make the bigger structures change direction and move ahead. We are all capable of being agile trim tabs that benefit our families, our communities, our businesses, and the world.

CHAPTER SEVEN

Improvisation

Resilient individuals and leaders are able to improvise—to create, innovate, and open up possibilities for the future. One way to achieve this is through seeking out mentorship and learning from others who have walked this path. Another way is through coaching, where powerful questions open new possibilities for the future.

Practical mentors teach you useful skills, while others share best practices for career, relationships, or spirituality. Top coaches ask questions and provide exercises to think about problems differently and innovate new solutions.

In his book *Man's Search for Meaning*, Viktor Frankl shares his experiences as a prisoner in Nazi concentration camps during World War II and finding a purpose in life to feel positive about and then imagining that outcome. Viktor was doing two things that researchers have since discovered are themes in resilient people and groups. The first is the skill of *reframing*. Frankl was not looking at his world unrealistically; he wasn't wearing rose-colored glasses or engaging in Pollyannic optimism. Instead, he developed a deep reverence for the meaning in the moment, and he remained curious in the midst of personal chaos. The second is the skill and practice of *improvisation*—to utilize what is available in the moment to move forward. Today, improvisation means the ability to find or create ways to stay in positive motion—like MacGyver using his remarkable resourcefulness to solve problems using mundane

materials available. For Frankl, finding and keeping a single strand of string to replace a broken shoelace meant having an additional resource to stay alive. Most challenges we face won't feel like life or death, but they weigh heavy on us nonetheless. And the pain of not knowing what to do or feeling under-resourced to meet the moment can be debilitating.

I have used improvisation regularly in my career. I have pivoted with confidence in several industries, because I felt resourced to solve problems using what was available at the time—including intuition drawn from difficult experiences of the past. An example of this was when I created Zoom recordings of new content to develop a virtual training platform and demo reel during a lull in speaking engagements. Of course, I could have waited to book a lot of speaking gigs first, but getting engagements often depends on developed and successful content. In this case, we improvised by switching the sequence of events to record content beforehand to test in the marketing and outreach to meeting planners. Reversing the order of initiatives is just one example of myriad ways to improvise solutions for business or life challenges.

At the highest level, improvisation starts with an internal knowing that leads to inspired answers. One way to do this is listening to your highest guide, maybe through meditation, prayer, or being in nature. (My form of meditation is surfing.)

CHAPTER EIGHT

Beyond Leadership

In addition to being individuals, we are all leaders. But moving beyond leadership means coming into your own. For business leaders, this may mean rebooting your corporate position, relaunching your existing business, or starting a new one. As a resilient leader, you lead with purpose. You easily enroll and onboard others. You distill your existing skills, knowledge, and experiences and refine them in your next level of growth. With your team, you do what it takes to reach the next goal.

George Henderson was born in 1897, and despite his mother's warning to his then wife-to-be to "find a man with more stable financial prospects," he went on to cofound the Sheraton hotel empire in 1933, right in the middle of the Great Depression. His people skills were said to be lacking, so he embarked on a path to turn his greatest weakness into an enduring legacy. Henderson studied the Dale Carnegie methods early on, including *How to Win Friends and Influence People* when it was first published in 1936.

Henderson was new to the hotel business in the 1930s, but he had learned something from the books he read and courses he studied about human nature. When purchasing their first hotels, Henderson was known to gather the staff (most of whom were worried they were about to be fired and replaced by the family and friends of those closest to the new owners) and tell them that he believed they knew best

how to do their jobs. He promised them the resources and encouragement to become the best they could be at their work. George's philosophy, according to his youngest daughter, Mitzi, was that "people will live up or down to our expectations of them." The guiding principle of his style of management was for employees (whom he referred to as "associates") to feel cared about. When renovating a property, the newly minted hotelier would reappoint and refurbish the staff's quarters, dining areas, bathrooms, and shower facilities first.

In other words, he would have substantial resources allocated to areas the paying public would never see. As the company grew and leaders were developed, the philosophy of building people up, not breaking them down, was mirrored in the speed that the Sheraton brand built its assets and prosperity.

Going beyond leadership doesn't mean that you stop leading. To the contrary, it means that you create other leaders who are individually and collectively greater than yourself. It means transcending the conventional roles we associate with someone in charge or something that has power over others. It is about modeling power that seeks no unfair advantage in relationship to another but simply shows the way forward by living and being the way forward. Beyond leadership involves going beyond title or convention to genuinely care about the people you influence—to teach by example, to mentor and guide, and to pass the torch and magnify the collective light in doing so. According to *A Course in Miracles*, by loving life (starting with your own existence), you will have what you truly want and therefore be capable of "[giving] it to the world by having it yourself."

At this stage, you've gained enough mastery to become the sovereign leader—of your life, your business, and your destiny. You create a life you love on an ongoing basis.

CHAPTER NINE

Harvest

By going on this journey, you begin to experience the harvest of your resilience. You can truthfully say, "I love my life!"

In the play *Hamilton*, George Washington says (or rather, sings), "I want to sit under my own vine and fig tree, a moment alone in the shade, at home in this nation we've made. One last time." He is getting ready to retire from public office after forty-five years of service to his country. He is ready to pass the torch to others who will have his mistakes and accomplishments to learn from. In Washington's farewell address, he warns a still-budding new nation to sow seeds of peace and cooperation among its citizenry, to carefully prune back rancor and divisiveness between our brothers and sisters, to ensure that we all may reap the harvest of lives and sit under our own vine and fig tree without fear or worry.

The relationship between cause and effect is visible in all things. We truly reap what we sow, and the essential question is not whether the events of one's life are good or bad, fair or unfair. Rather, the question is if you are plowing a field by intention and design to produce a harvest of your own self-determination or if you're leaving the harvest to other people or circumstances by default. Like Washington, we must take responsibility for our destiny and seek to create our bounty and harvest in the shade.

By loving your life now instead of waiting for life to give you reasons to agree, you reap the benefits, both personal and professional. The personal bounty includes harmony, freedom, a sense of life's mission being fulfilled, and alignment with your own inner guidance. Business and professional bounties include clearer focus; new opportunities; greater financial returns; higher levels of performance; more innovation, agility, and relevance in the marketplace; and greater impact in the world. Corporate harvests include more profitability, aligned investors, strong brand presence, abundant good-will, impeccability, employee loyalty and longevity, momentum, market prescience, agility, innovation, resilience in the face of challenge and disruption, and clarity in the face of uncertainty.

CONCLUSION

Grace

Since starting this journey, you have begun experiencing more harmony, freedom, and abundance. You are growing as a resilient leader.

John Wooden was one of college basketball's greatest coaches. Heck, Wooden is considered one of the very best coaches who ever lived. Why? What made him tick, and how was he so much more successful than thousands of others who came before and after him? The answer: *grace*. Coach Wooden was the elegant embodiment of his methods and practices; a great athlete in his own right, a student of life's trilogy of mind, body, and spirit, Wooden was also renowned for his short, simple inspirational messages to his players, including his Pyramid of Success. His efforts were often directed at how to be a success in life as well as on the basketball court. Wooden's twenty-nine-year coaching career and overwhelmingly positive critical acclaim created a legacy of great interest in not only sports but in business, personal success, and organizational leadership as well.

Grace is one of those words and concepts that reaches all our senses. It's mental and physical, emotional, and spiritual. Grace can be a poise and a presence all at once. The word is defined in religious and secular contexts, yet it defies exactitude—it's ineffable, actually. But what we know of it, we can see and hear and smell and taste and feel inside. Grace is us being in tune with our true essence and being and sharing that presence with others. Coach Wooden was soft-spoken but hardly shy. He was in alignment with himself and his highest calling to serve his student-athletes. He assessed himself and those he led by the same standards and developed resilient individuals and teams. His successes were not immune from the common challenges of injury and ego, yet his teams prevailed again and again. In fact, the "Wizard of Westwood" won ten NCAA national championships in a twelve-year period as head coach of the UCLA Bruins, including a record seven in a row. No other team has ever won more than four consecutively.

Resilience is our grace. To live and to grow another day is not just how we survive but how we *win* at life!

I now invite you to share your transformation with me and our community. If you have not already taken the Resilience Assessment, I invite you to take it now. I also invite you to join our online I Love My Life community and discussions so you can shore up your reserves and recharge. Once you are your own captain, you can build teams or crews in your life and business that operate on cultures of resilience.

Change never ends, and winds never cease. The question is, will you love your life, no matter how the winds blow? When you learn to love *your* life, you experience grace, and life will love you back in many unexpected ways. You will live an impactful life, with no one left behind.

Mental Health Resources

If you or someone you love is experiencing mental health struggles, please know there are resources out there to help you more than this book or any book could. Here are but a few that are ready to assist you today:

- If you've considered any type of harm to yourself, the National Suicide Prevention Lifeline at 800-273-8255 offers 24/7 support.

- If you aren't ready for such a call yet, text! You can use the Crisis Text Line. Text HOME to 741741 for 24/7, anonymous, free crisis counseling.

- If you are ready to seek out treatment but don't know where to start, go to FindTreatment.gov. They can help you find a treatment provider for mental illness in any form, including substance use disorders, addiction, and depression.

* Note these resources are for U.S. readers, but most countries have their own similar form of support.

About the Author

Adam Markel is the number one *Wall Street Journal*, *USA Today*, *Los Angeles Times*, and *Publishers Weekly* bestselling author of *Pivot: The Art and Science of Reinventing Your Career and Life* and *Soul Over Matter: Ancient and Modern Wisdom and Practical Techniques to Create Unlimited Abundance*.

A leading international speaker, Adam reaches tens of thousands of audience members worldwide each year with his message of resilience. An attorney, entrepreneur, and transformational speaker, Adam is a sought-after business leader who inspires, empowers, and guides people to achieve massive and lasting personal and professional growth.

Adam hosts *The Conscious Pivot* podcast, where he shares his insights on pivoting in today's fast-paced market while interviewing experts, innovators, and influencers in business and life. Adam is also CEO of the More Love Media Group, a company dedicated to empowering individuals and businesses to reimagine, refocus, and capitalize on change in order to thrive in a world where constant disruption is the new normal.

Before his pivot to the world of personal and business development, Adam founded a multimillion-dollar law firm specializing in finance, commercial, and employment litigation. Over the course of his eighteen-year practice, he acted as counsel in more than one thousand matters with hundreds of clients, including Citibank and HSBC.

After a midlife crisis became a midlife calling, Adam reinvented his career and has since trained and led programs for more than one hundred thousand people around the globe in the areas of business and entre-preneurship, finances, health, spirituality, and relation-ships. As a self-proclaimed "recovered attorney," he has shared his unique content and heart-led leadership style on four continents, in dozens of countries, and throughout hundreds of cities. He is an expert at leading transformational events and filling them to capacity, and he has successfully delivered sold-out training events around the world.

Adam's powerful and practical talks offer a unique bridge between self-development and business mastery. His speeches are crafted to inspire, empower, and guide people to achieve a greater impact through higher levels of awareness, authenticity, and action. He's been a keynote speaker and workshop facilitator for Fortune 500 companies, and he's shared the stage with the likes of Michael J. Fox, Jack Canfield, and Tony Robbins. Adam was honored to become a member of the prestigious Transformational Leadership Council and Association of Transformational Leaders.

As a recognized expert in the integration of business and personal development, Adam has been interviewed by many outlets, including *Entrepreneur* magazine, *Inc.* magazine, American Express, *Forbes*,

Fox News, *Newsday*, the *Los Angeles Times*, the *New York Post*, the *Observer*, and the *Wall Street Journal.*

Adam stands out as a heart-centered leader, father of four, and husband of more than thirty years. He teaches using the same principles that transformed his past pain and struggle as a workaholic New York City litigation attorney into a life of inspiration, purpose, creative expression, and success. He is a visionary and an artist of reinvention.

The I Love My Life Challenge distills the most essential wisdom from Adam's unique perspective into a treatise that answers the most pressing questions facing business and humanity today. In addition, Adam offers simple, easy, and quick practices to create resilience—in a matter of moments.

For more information and media assets, visit adammarkel.com and adammarkel.onlinepresskit247.com/.

NEW! Only from Simple Truths®

IGNITE READS
spark impact in just one hour

IGNITE READS IS A NEW SERIES OF 1-HOUR READS WRITTEN BY WORLD-RENOWNED EXPERTS!

These captivating books will help you become the best version of yourself, allowing for new opportunities in your personal and professional life. Accelerate your career and expand your knowledge with these powerful books written on today's hottest ideas.

TRENDING BUSINESS AND PERSONAL GROWTH TOPICS

 Read in an hour or less

 Leading experts and authors

 Bold design and captivating content

EXCLUSIVELY AVAILABLE ON SIMPLETRUTHS.COM

Need a training framework?
Engage your team with discussion guides and PowerPoints for training events or meetings.

Want your own branded editions?
Express gratitude, appreciation, and instill positive perceptions to staff or clients by adding your organization's logo to your edition of the book.

Add a supplemental visual experience
to any meeting, training, or event.

Contact us for special corporate discounts!
(800) 900-3427 x247 or
simpletruths@sourcebooks.com

LOVED WHAT YOU READ AND WANT MORE?

Sign up today and be the FIRST to receive advance copies of Simple Truths® NEW releases written and signed by expert authors. Enjoy a complete package of supplemental materials that can help you host or lead a successful event. This high-value program will uplift you to be the best version of yourself!

SIMPLE TRUTHS

ELITE CLUB

ONE MONTH. ONE BOOK. ONE HOUR.

Your monthly dose of motivation, inspiration, and personal growth.